EUROPEAN COUNTRIES TODAY
PORTUGAL

EUROPEAN COUNTRIES TODAY

TITLES IN THE SERIES

Austria	**Italy**
Belgium	**Netherlands**
Czech Republic	**Poland**
Denmark	**Portugal**
France	**Spain**
Germany	**Sweden**
Greece	**United Kingdom**
Ireland	**European Union Facts & Figures**

EUROPEAN COUNTRIES TODAY
PORTUGAL

Dominic J. Ainsley

MASON CREST

Mason Crest
450 Parkway Drive, Suite D
Broomall, Pennsylvania PA 19008
(866) MCP-BOOK (toll free)

Copyright © 2019 by Mason Crest, an imprint of National Highlights, Inc. All rights reserved. No part of this publication may be reproduced or transmitted in any form or by any means, electronic or mechanical, including photocopying, recording, taping, or any information storage and retrieval system, without permission in writing from the publisher.

First printing
9 8 7 6 5 4 3 2 1

ISBN: 978-1-4222-3990-2
Series ISBN: 978-1-4222-3977-3
ebook ISBN: 978-1-4222-7805-5

Cataloging-in-Publication Data on file with the Library of Congress.

Printed in the United States of America

Cover images
Main: *Lisbon's skyline.*
Left: *Pastéis de Nata (Portuguese custard tarts).*
Center: *The Algarve.*
Right: *Harvesting grapes in Portugal.*

QR CODES AND LINKS TO THIRD-PARTY CONTENT

You may gain access to certain third-party content ("Third- Party Sites") by scanning and using the QR Codes that appear in this publication (the "QR Codes"). We do not operate or control in any respect any information, products, or services on such Third-Party Sites linked to by us via the QR Codes included in this publication, and we assume no responsibility for any materials you may access using the QR Codes. Your use of the QR Codes may be subject to terms, limitations, or restrictions set forth in the applicable terms of use or otherwise established by the owners of the Third-Party Sites. Our linking to such Third-Party Sites via the QR Codes does not imply an endorsement or sponsorship of such Third-Party Sites or the information, products, or services offered on or through the Third-Party Sites, nor does it imply an endorsement or sponsorship of this publication by the owners of such Third-Party Sites.

CONTENTS

Portugal at a Glance	6
Chapter 1: Portugal's Geography & Landscape	11
Chapter 2: The Government & History of Portugal	23
Chapter 3: The Portuguese Economy	39
Chapter 4: Citizens of Portugal: People, Customs & Culture	49
Chapter 5: The Famous Cities of Portugal	63
Chapter 6: A Bright Future for Portugal	81
Chronology	90
Further Reading & Internet Resources	91
Index	92
Picture Credits & Author	96

KEY ICONS TO LOOK FOR:

Words to Understand: These words with their easy-to-understand definitions will increase the reader's understanding of the text while building vocabulary skills.

Sidebars: This boxed material within the main text allows readers to build knowledge, gain insights, explore possibilities, and broaden their perspectives by weaving together additional information to provide realistic and holistic perspectives.

Educational Videos: Readers can view videos by scanning our QR codes, providing them with additional content to supplement the text. Examples include news coverage, moments in history, speeches, iconic sports moments, and much more!

Text-Dependent Questions: These questions send the reader back to the text for more careful attention to the evidence presented there.

Research Projects: Readers are pointed toward areas of further inquiry connected to each chapter. Suggestions are provided for projects that encourage deeper research and analysis.

PORTUGAL AT A GLANCE

MAP OF EUROPE

The Geography of Portugal

Location: southwestern Europe, bordering the North Atlantic Ocean, west of Spain

Area: slightly smaller than Virginia
 total: 35,555 square miles (92,090 sq. km)
 land: 35,316 square miles (91,470 sq. km)
 water: 239 square miles (620 sq. km)

Borders: Spain 760 miles (1,224 km)

Climate: maritime temperate; cool and rainy in north, warmer and drier in south

Terrain: the west-flowing Tagus River divides the country: the north is mountainous toward the interior, while the south is characterized by rolling plains

Elevation extremes:
 lowest point: Atlantic 0 feet (0 m)
 highest point: Ponta do Pico (Pico or Pico Alto) on Ilha do Pico in the Azores 7,713 feet (2,351 m)

Natural hazards: Azores subject to severe earthquakes

Source: www.cia.gov 2017

PORTUGAL AT A GLANCE

Flag of Portugal

Portugal is situated on the Atlantic coastline of the Iberian Peninsula.

Important for its maritime history, it was the first European country to send a ship around the world. Portugal joined the European Union in 1986, but remains comparatively poor in relation to other European countries. The flag dates from 1910 when Portugal became a republic, with red symbolizing the revolution that took place and green standing for hope and the sea. The central shield dates back to the twelfth century, created when Alfonso I defeated five Moorish kings at the Battle of Ourique. The coat of arms is set on an armillary sphere, a nautical instrument that recalls the time of the Portuguese maritime voyages of exploration.

ABOVE: *People dining outside in the capital city of Lisbon.*

EUROPEAN COUNTRIES TODAY: PORTUGAL

The People of Portugal

Population: 10,839,514
Ethnic Groups: homogeneous Mediterranean stock; citizens of black African descent who immigrated to the mainland during decolonization number less than 100,000; since 1990, East Europeans have entered Portugal
Age Structure:
    0–14 years: 15.34%
    15–24 years: 11.36%
    25–54 years: 41.72%
    55–64 years: 12.18%
    65 years and over: 19.4%
Population Growth Rate: 0.04%
Birth Rate: 9 births/1,000 population
Death Rate: 11.1 deaths/1,000 population
Migration Rate: 2.5 migrant(s)/1,000 population
Infant Mortality Rate: 4.3 deaths/1,000 live births
Life Expectancy at Birth:
    Total Population: 79.4 years
    Male: 76.2 years
    Female: 82.9 years
Total Fertility Rate: 1.53 children born/woman
Religions: Roman Catholic 81%, other Christian 3.3%, other (includes Jewish, Muslim, other) 0.6%, none 6.8%, unspecified 8.3%
Languages: Portuguese (official), Mirandese (official, but locally used)
Literacy rate: 95.7%

Source: www.cia.gov 2017

Words to Understand

empire: A group of territories or peoples under one ruler.

fertile: Land producing many plants or crops.

trade routes: Routes followed by traders.

BELOW: *The Peneda-Gerês National Park is in northern Portugal, near the Spanish border. Its rugged hills are home to deer, wolves, and golden eagles.*

Chapter One
PORTUGAL'S GEOGRAPHY & LANDSCAPE

In recent years, Portugal has often been overshadowed by its larger neighbor, Spain. However, it was once a wealthy and powerful nation, ruling an empire that stretched across the globe. Although it has lost much of that glory, it remains a colorful and fascinating country in modern times.

The smaller of the only two countries to occupy the Iberian Peninsula (the other being Spain), Portugal has an area of 35,555 square miles (92,090

ABOVE: *The Fort of São João Baptista das Berlengas, is located on the west coast of Portugal, on the largest island of the Berlengas archipelago.*

PORTUGAL'S GEOGRAPHY & LANDSCAPE

Educational Video

This short video provides a brief insight into the geography of the Azores, Portugal's Atlantic islands. Scan the QR code with your phone to watch!

ABOVE: *The beautiful coast of the Algarve is on the Atlantic coast.*

12

EUROPEAN COUNTRIES TODAY: PORTUGAL

ABOVE: *Lagoa Comprida is the largest lake in the Serra da Estrela Natural Park.*

square kilometers), which makes it slightly smaller than the state of Indiana. The nation also includes two Atlantic island chains: the Azores and Madeira Islands.

North, Center, and South: Different Lands

Although it only measures 350 miles (560 kilometers) from north to south, Portugal is divided geographically between these areas. The central region of the country contains its capital, Lisbon. Geographically, this area has pine forests and gently rolling land. In the north, the land tens to be more **fertile** and better suited for growing crops such as corn and grapes. This region also contains several rivers and forests. For these reasons, the north is more populated than the south. Many of its cities are located on the rivers, which provide water and **trade routes**, both historically and today.

13

PORTUGAL'S GEOGRAPHY & LANDSCAPE

ABOVE: *Quinta do Lorde on the island of Madeira. Madeira is an autonomous region of Portugal. It is an archipelago comprising four islands off the African coast.*

The mountains of the north can be impressive: the highest peak in continental Portugal, Torre, is 6,450 feet (1,993 meters) high. This mountain is part of the Serra da Estrela range, the highest in the country.

In the south, in the area known as the Alentejo, the land is more arid and is unable to grow as many crops, though olives, oranges, and figs are able to survive. The land is mostly made up of hills and plains. Even farther south is the Algarve, which is the driest and hottest part of Portugal.

The Islands

In the early fifteenth century, two island chains, or archipelagos, were discovered by Portugal and incorporated into the country. The Azores and Madeira Islands are both located in the northern Atlantic Ocean and are inhabited by people from the mainland of Portugal, along with others from various European countries.

EUROPEAN COUNTRIES TODAY: PORTUGAL

The Azores consist of nine islands that are peopled, as well as several islands that are uninhabited. They are located 800 miles (289 kilometers) to the west of mainland Portugal. The islands are generally forested, except for the beaches that form their coasts. The Madeira Islands, which are farther from the Iberian Peninsula, are closer to Africa than Portugal. The islands' coasts are rockier than those on the Azores, but their interiors are just as green and lush.

Volcanoes formed most of the islands. Volcanic activity helped to create the 370-mile (600-kilometer) stretch of Azorean Islands. Many of the islands are home to tall mountains, such as the volcano on Pico Island, the highest peak in all of Portugal.

ABOVE: Lagoa das Sete Cidades is a twin-lake complex situated in the crater of a dormant volcano on the Portuguese archipelago of the Azores.

PORTUGAL'S GEOGRAPHY & LANDSCAPE

ABOVE: *The rocky Atlantic coastline near Praia da Marinha, which is close to the town of Lagoa in the Algarve region.*

EUROPEAN COUNTRIES TODAY: PORTUGAL

Coasts and Rivers

Much of Portuguese life centers around the 1,115-mile (1,793-kilometer) coastline. Historically, this easy access to the sea fueled Portugal's expansion and exploration.

Ten major rivers flow through Portugal. Since it provides a trade route to and from Spain and Portugal, one of the most important in the north is the Duoro River. The Tagus River, the longest river in the country, winds its way through Lisbon. Since it is deep enough to provide passage for large cargo ships, it is considered the most important commercial river in the nation.

Portugal's climate can vary from region to region but, in general, it tends to temperate. In the south, summers can be extremely hot, especially in the southern region of Algarve, but the region usually remains comfortably warm throughout the rest of the year; the average summer temperature is 78 degrees F (25 degrees C). The north experiences slightly cooler weather and has a

ABOVE: *The old town of Porto on the Duoro River.*

17

PORTUGAL'S GEOGRAPHY & LANDSCAPE

ABOVE: The Iberian wolf is a subspecies of grey wolf that inhabits the forest and plains of northern Portugal.

EUROPEAN COUNTRIES TODAY: PORTUGAL

Iberian Lynx

The Iberian lynx is a medium-sized wild cat species native to the Iberian Peninsula. Formerly considered to be a subspecies of the Eurasian lynx, the Iberian lynx is now classified as a separate species. The Iberian lynx is endangered, although conservation measures has increased its numbers. Lynx populations, habitats, and food sources are carefully monitored. It preys on the European rabbit for its food, however, declining populations of rabbits due to disease has caused a food shortage for the lynx. This extremely efficient hunter uses fine-tuned stealth and pounce techniques to bring down prey, delivering a fatal bite to the neck of an unsuspecting rabbit. The Iberian lynx has a tawny colored spotted and short fur, a short body, long legs, a short tail, a small head with tufted ears and facial whiskers.

distinct winter season, characterized by rain and colder temperatures. Portugal's average winter temperature is about 61 degrees F (16 degrees C). In the higher mountains, snowfall is not uncommon.

The coastal regions tend to be cooler, since the ocean moderates the weather. The Azores, surrounded by the sea, have moderate temperatures that change little throughout the year, ranging from 55 degrees F (13 degrees C) to 76 degrees F (25 degrees C). The Madeira Islands have similar temperatures.

Flora and Fauna

Much of Portugal is covered with forests. More varieties of trees are found in the north, including pine, elm, poplar, and oak. Cork oak is the most common

PORTUGAL'S GEOGRAPHY & LANDSCAPE

type of tree growing in the south. Other plants besides trees grow in Portugal, including orchids, lavender, rosemary, and broom.

The animals of Portugal are generally typical to the rest of the Iberian Peninsula. Deer, wild goats, hares, rabbits, and several types of birds are common sights. Wolves, foxes, and lynx make the mountains their homes. Portugal is also home to a number of animals that are considered endangered. These include the whale, the monk seal, and the northern right whale.

Environmental Concerns

Like most countries, Portugal must balance its prosperity and growth with the need to protect and preserve the environment. As its population has grown, people have pushed into wild areas, destroying habitats in order to use them for

ABOVE: *The Alqueva reservoir and dam were created by flooding an area by the Guadiana River. This caused much controversy as it destroyed many natural habitats for wildlife.*

EUROPEAN COUNTRIES TODAY: PORTUGAL

farming, housing, or other human needs. In 2001, the construction of an artificial lake on the Guadiana River was finished. Many people opposed the project because of the invasive construction that was necessary.

Deforestation is also a problem. Old-growth forests, or woods that have never been cut down, are becoming rare and only exist in the more remote parts of the mountains. Portugal has set aside parts of the country for the conservation of these forests, as well as other rare habitats and wildlife. These areas are divided into a national park, twelve natural parks, and several natural reserves, natural monuments, and protected landscapes.

Some problems dealing with the environment are beyond the people of Portugal's control. In 2017, the country was victim to a series of forest fires that burned a massive area of land and killed sixty-two people.

Text-Dependent Questions

1. Which two countries occupy the Iberian Peninsula?

2. How many of the Azores Islands are peopled?

3. What is the longest river in Portugal?

Research Project

Write an essay on the natural wildlife in Portugal and explain what steps Portugal has taken to protect its flora, fauna, and natural areas.

Words to Understand

Lusitanians: Peoples of an ancient region and Roman province in the Iberian Peninsula, corresponding generally to modern Portugal.

peninsula: An area of land almost completely surrounded by water.

Visigoths: Members of the western division of the Goths.

BELOW: There is evidence of human habitation along the Tagus River dating back to 5500 BCE.

Chapter Two
THE GOVERNMENT & HISTORY OF PORTUGAL

Portugal has a long, rich history that begins in prehistoric times and spans many centuries. Its history has helped shape Portugal's culture and who its people are today.

Early Portugal

Scientists have speculated that people have inhabited Portugal for the past 500,000 years. Hunter-gatherers, who lived along river valleys, were the main residents for much of the earliest part of this time. Advanced settlements—fortified villages in the Tagus Valley—have been discovered that date back to 5500 BCE.

In 700 BCE, the peninsula was settled by a group of people known as the Celts, who arrived from central Europe. They assimilated into the local culture of the people already living in the area, forming the Celt-Iberians, or Lusitanians. Many other groups followed, including the Phoenicians, Greeks, and Romans, who first invaded the peninsula in 219 BCE. The Visigoths, a Germanic tribe, conquered almost all of the peninsula in the fifth century CE. These invaders came from the area around what is now Germany.

ABOVE: A medieval depiction of the Moors in Iberia.

The Golden Age of the Moors and Christian Reconquest

The Moors, a group of Muslims, were

23

THE GOVERNMENT & HISTORY OF PORTUGAL

Educational Video

Portugal: powerful history, exceptional cuisine, and cinematic scenery.

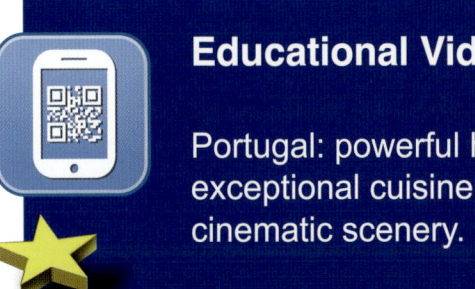

ABOVE: *The Castle of the Moors is a hilltop medieval castle located in the municipality of Sintra. The castle dates back to the eighth century.*

EUROPEAN COUNTRIES TODAY: PORTUGAL

ABOVE: *The Algarve town of Silves. The Moorish castle and cathedral are in the background. Although the castle is Roman in origin, the castle we can see today, dates to the eighth century. Silves is a beautiful town, full of interesting buildings.*

one of the most important influences on the Iberian Peninsula. Arriving from northern Africa, they began their occupation of present-day Portugal and Spain in 711 CE. They conquered most of the peninsula, except for one small piece of land in the northwest.

The Moors left a lasting mark on Portugal that is still evident today, especially in the Algarve in the south, which the Moors preferred to the rest of the country because of its hot, dry conditions that reminded them of their homelands. Their centuries-long inhabitance of the area, which they referred to as *al-Andalus*, meant that the cultures of the Moors and the local Portuguese natives mixed together, forming a unique blend of customs, architecture, food, and language that could only be found on the Iberian Peninsula.

THE GOVERNMENT & HISTORY OF PORTUGAL

Dating Systems and Their Meaning

You might be accustomed to seeing dates expressed with the abbreviations BC or AD, as in the year 1000 BC or the year AD 1900. For centuries, this dating system has been the most common in the Western world. However, since BC and AD are based on Christianity (BC stands for Before Christ and AD stands for anno Domini, Latin for "in the year of our Lord"), many people now prefer to use abbreviations that people from all religions can be comfortable using. The abbreviations BCE (meaning Before Common Era) and CE (meaning Common Era) mark time in the same way (for example, 1000 BC is the same year as 1000 BCE, and AD 1900 is the same year as 1900 CE), but BCE and CE do not have the same religious overtones as BC and AD.

ABOVE: *Porto on the Douro River fell under the control of the Moors in 716, following the invasion of the Iberian Peninsula in 711.*

EUROPEAN COUNTRIES TODAY: PORTUGAL

Under the Moors, peace and prosperity were brought to Portugal. Most of the natives were easily converted to Islam, although religious toleration was practiced. Education, the arts, and industry all leapt ahead, transforming Portugal into a center of culture and trade.

Moorish rule was challenged early on by Christians from the County of Portugal to the north (who had remained unconquered). They were determined to retake the south and slowly regained control of the territory that makes up Portugal today. Their war of reconquest lasted for almost four hundred years, finally ending in 1249.

The Formation of Portugal

The king of Astúrias-León, who had gained power after fighting the Moors, appointed nobles to rule the province of Portucalense. Soon, rule over this area became a hereditary title. One count, Afonso Henriques, proclaimed himself king of Portugal and was eventually recognized by the king of Astúrias-León in 1143.

Afonso Henriques and his heirs conquered the remaining Muslims, and over the period of about a century, they expanded the borders of the kingdom to form what is now the familiar shape of Portugal.

ABOVE: *Statue of Afonso Henriques, the first king of Portugal and founder of the Portuguese nation, in Guimarães.*

THE GOVERNMENT & HISTORY OF PORTUGAL

ABOVE: *King João was the king of Portugal and the Algarve between 1385 and 1433.*

EUROPEAN COUNTRIES TODAY: PORTUGAL

Expansion

In the fifteenth century, Portugal began to explore the oceans and beyond, ushering in a period of glory. The need for new trade routes, as well as the fact that the country had expanded as far as it could on the Iberian Peninsula, meant that Portugal had to look to the seas. Portugal also possessed advanced nautical knowledge and was in a good position for naval exploration.

The major force behind Portugal's exploration was Prince Henry the Navigator, the son of King João (John). Under his direction and financial help, the ships of Portugal were able to create new trade routes and a new empire. At its greatest extent, the empire reached India, Brazil, and Africa.

During the 1400s, Portugal was one of the most powerful countries in the world. The monarchy became the richest in Europe, and they established the country as a center for trade.

The Inquisition

Despite the prosperity that Portugal seemed to have, many problems lurked beneath the surface. Social inequality continued, and freedom of speech was not encouraged. One of the most famous examples of this is the Inquisition. This repression of the freedom of religion took place in Portugal, as well as in Spain.

In 1539, the king of Portugal, João III, set up a Court of Inquisition, which tried and condemned 1,400 people to death for heresy. Many of those sentenced to death were Jews who had already converted to Christianity, but who were suspected of still practicing Judaism.

ABOVE: *King João III was monarch from 1521 to 1557.*

THE GOVERNMENT & HISTORY OF PORTUGAL

The Decline of Portugal

The empire's wealth and power depended on the strength of the monarch. After the death of João III, who had been a powerful king, Portugal's glory declined because of the lack of another strong king.

In 1580, Spain invaded and annexed Portugal, making Spain's Philip II, who was crowned Felipe I, king of Portugal. Under Spain, the country became too weak to hold on to its empire, so it lost much of the land it had held in Asia and Africa. Portugal was able to regain its independence in 1640, but not its former power.

EUROPEAN COUNTRIES TODAY: PORTUGAL

ABOVE: An antique map, published in Portugal in 1623, showing the Spanish and Portuguese maritime and colonial empire.

Democracy Takes Hold

As in other European countries, republicanism became a widespread idea in Portugal in the 1800s. The recent French Revolution helped to spread the desire for democracy, as did propaganda that made its way into Portugal. In 1812, a secret society, the Sinédrio, was formed to pass on revolutionary ideas.

In 1822, a constitutional monarchy was created. While the king still held power, he shared it with a legislative body (the Chamber of Deputies) and a court system. The new constitution created a division in society between those

THE GOVERNMENT & HISTORY OF PORTUGAL

ABOVE: King Miguel I.

who supported it and those who wanted to go back to a complete monarchy.

Later, another constitution, the Constitutional Charter, was created, giving the king more power. However, in 1828, King Miguel I declared that this constitution was null. A later king, Pedro II restored it. In 1910, the monarchy was completely abolished after demonstrations and unrest, and a democratic republic was set up in a bloodless revolution.

Problems with Democracy

For the next fifteen years, Portugal had a troubled and unstable government. The outbreak of World War I did not help the struggling country. In 1916, 40,000 Portuguese soldiers were sent to fight with the Allies. Unfortunately, they were not well trained or well equipped, and many of the men were killed in the fighting. Learning from its mistakes, Portugal remained neutral in World War II. However, it allowed the Allies to build air and naval bases on Portuguese territory.

Three attempts were made to overthrow the government after democracy was established. One, in 1926, led to dictatorship under António de Oliveira Salazar. His reign was not as oppressive as others of the time, and even included some improvements on society, such as

EUROPEAN COUNTRIES TODAY: PORTUGAL

ABOVE: António de Oliveira Salazar in 1940.

THE GOVERNMENT & HISTORY OF PORTUGAL

giving women the right to vote. However, people were still unable to freely express their opinions, and all political parties were banned. Salazar's government ended upon his death in 1968.

Under Salazar, Portugal's economy grew very slowly. By the middle of the twentieth century, the country was clearly behind those of the rest of Europe and was admitted late to the United Nations, in 1955. After Salazar's death, a successful revolt deposed his successor, Marcello Caetano, and set up a new, democratic government.

There was also unrest in many of Portugal's remaining colonies, especially those in Africa. Portugal lost money dealing with revolts and wars that eventually ended in independence for all of Portugal's colonies in 1974 and 1975.

ABOVE: Marcello Caetano.

Modern Portugal

Over the last few decades, Portugal has slowly recovered some of its lost power and has entered the global community. In 1986, the country joined the European Community, which would eventually become the European Union (EU). It also became a member of the European Monetary Union in 1999.

The current government is much more stable than it has been in the past. The president is elected every five years and can

ABOVE: António Costa has been prime minister of Portugal since 2015.

EUROPEAN COUNTRIES TODAY: PORTUGAL

appoint the prime minister. The Council of Ministers makes up the rest of the executive branch. The legislative body is made up of the 230-member Assembly of the Republic, a unicameral house. The government also includes a court system, with the Supreme Court being the highest court. The government has been working hard in recent years to improve the country's rapidly growing economy.

The current prime minister of Portugal is António Costa, who came into office in November 2015. Costa's Socialist Party did not win the election outright, but he managed to form a coalition of left-wing parties. After years of austerity imposed on Portugal following a bailout from the International Monetary Fund, Costa's anti-austerity policies were somewhat controversial. However, within a year of taking power, the Portuguese economy started to recover and is still growing today.

Text-Dependent Questions

1. Where did the Moors come from?

2. Who was the major force behind Portugal's exploration of other lands?

3. When did Portugal's last colonies gain independence?

Research Project

Portugal set up colonies in many parts of the world. Research and write a report on where the colonies were and how those countries were affected by Portugal.

35

THE GOVERNMENT & HISTORY OF PORTUGAL

The Formation of the European Union (EU)

The EU is a confederation of European nations that continues to grow. As of 2017, there are twenty-eight official members. Several other candidates are also waiting for approval. All countries that enter the EU agree to follow common laws about foreign security policies. They also agree to cooperate on legal matters that go on within the EU. The European Council meets to discuss all international matters and make decisions about them. Each country's own concerns and interests are important, though. And apart from legal and financial issues, the EU tries to uphold values such as peace, human dignity, freedom, and equality.

All member countries remain autonomous. This means that they generally keep their own laws and regulations. The idea for a union among European nations was first mentioned after World War II. The war had devastated much of Europe, both physically and financially. In 1950, the French foreign minister suggested that France and West Germany combine their coal and steel industries under one authority. Both countries would have control over the

ABOVE: The entrance to the European Union Parliament Building in Brussels.

EUROPEAN COUNTRIES TODAY: PORTUGAL

Member Countries

Austria	Greece	Romania
Belgium	Hungary	Slovakia
Bulgaria	Ireland	Slovenia
Croatia	Italy	Spain
Cyprus	Latvia	Sweden
Czech Republic	Lithuania	United Kingdom
Denmark	Luxembourg	*(Brexit: For the time*
Estonia	Malta	*being, the United*
Finland	Netherlands	*Kingdom remains a full*
France	Poland	*member of the EU.)*
Germany	Portugal	

industries. This would help them become more financially stable. It would also make war between the countries much more difficult. The idea was interesting to other European countries as well. In 1951, France, West Germany, Belgium, Luxembourg, the Netherlands, and Italy signed the Treaty of Paris, creating the European Coal and Steel Community. These six countries would become the core of the EU.

In 1957, these same countries signed the Treaties of Rome, creating the European Economic Community. In 1965, the Merger Treaty formed the European Community. Finally, in 1992, the Maastricht Treaty was signed. This treaty defined the European Union. It gave a framework for expanding the EU's political role, particularly in the area of foreign and security policy. It would also replace national currencies with the euro. The next year, the treaty went into effect. At that time, the member countries included the original six plus another six who had joined during the 1970s and '80s.

In the following years, the EU would take more steps to form a single market for its members. This would make joining the union even more advantageous. In addition to enlargement, the EU is steadily becoming more integrated through its own policies for closer cooperation between member states.

Words to Understand

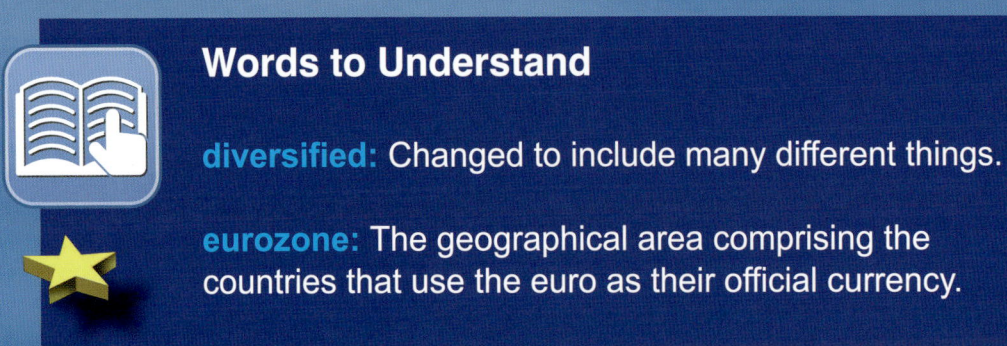

diversified: Changed to include many different things.

eurozone: The geographical area comprising the countries that use the euro as their official currency.

projections: An estimate of what might happen in the future based on what is happening now.

BELOW: *Vineyards in the Douro Valley where grapes are grown to make port, a fortified wine, which is exported all over the world.*

Chapter Three
THE PORTUGUESE ECONOMY

Portugal has become a **diversified** and increasingly service-based economy since joining the European Community in 1986. The country qualified to become a part of the **eurozone** in 1998 and began circulating the euro on January 1, 2002.

During the 1990s, the economy grew faster than the EU average, but that began to change in the first decade of the twenty-first century when Portugal's economy began to contract. Today, however, Portugal's economy is growing again and surpassing many EU and IMF **projections**.

ABOVE: *The fishing harbor at Sesimbra, which is situated on the west coast, at the mouth of the Sado River. Fishing is an important part of the Portuguese economy.*

THE PORTUGUESE ECONOMY

ABOVE: The climate of the Algarve is suitable for growing oranges and other citrus fruits. This orange grove is also being used to graze sheep.

EUROPEAN COUNTRIES TODAY: PORTUGAL

Agriculture

In today's world, most countries have begun to rely less and less on farming to sustain their economies. Portugal's economy, on the other hand, still relies heavily on agriculture. About 9 percent of the population is involved with farming, forestry, or fishing. Most of the land grows olives, wheat, corn, grapes, potatoes, and tomatoes. Fruits, especially citrus fruits like oranges, are also grown.

The products made from these crops are sold throughout the world, as well as locally in Portugal. Portuguese wines and olive oils are especially well known.

Despite the number of people and land dedicated to agriculture, it provides Portugal with less than 3 percent of its gross domestic product (GDP). This is because not enough modern technology is used to get the most out of agriculture. The solution to this problem is one of Portugal's long-term goals.

ABOVE: An olive grove near the town of Évora. Évora is the capital of Portugal's south-central Alentejo region.

THE PORTUGUESE ECONOMY

Growing Industry and Trade

Manufacturing and industry have grown in Portugal during the twentieth and twenty-first centuries, especially after it joined the EU. Although it still tends to lag behind other Western European countries, it is slowly establishing itself in industries such as automobile production, electronics, paper manufacturing, and food processing.

Portugal trades mostly with other EU member states. It imports most of its products from EU members such as Spain, Italy, the United Kingdom (UK), Germany, and France. It exports its products to Germany, France, and Spain. Portugal's primary exports are agricultural goods, taking advantage of its supply of cork trees, other wood, and fruit. It imports machinery, cars, oil, and textiles.

Natural Resources

One of Portugal's greatest resources is wood. Portugal alone provides the world with over half of its supply of cork oak wood. About 36 percent of the land, particularly in the north, is covered in trees, including pine trees, holm oak, cork oak, and eucalyptus.

Mining, although not a major industry, still occurs in Portugal. Tungsten, uranium, and tin are the most abundant minerals that are mined. Coal and copper are also mined.

Educational Video

The best fish in the world comes from Portugal. An insight into the life of a local fisherman.

EUROPEAN COUNTRIES TODAY: PORTUGAL

ABOVE: The cork tree is extraordinary in that it has a thick, rugged bark that can be removed every eight years or so to produce cork, mainly for the wine industry. The harvesting does not harm the tree; in fact, no trees are cut down during the process. Only the bark is removed, and a new layer of cork regrows, making it a renewable resource.

THE PORTUGUESE ECONOMY

Transportation

Transportation has seen a huge push in growth in recent years. Portugal's highways are modern and extensive, connecting most areas of the country as well as linking it to Spain. The Metro, a type of subway system, can be found in Lisbon and Porto. This public form of transportation is fast and can carry passengers from one part of the city to another fairly inexpensively.

Seaports and airports are also important centers of transportation for the movement of goods and people through and around Portugal. The thousands of miles of coast in the west of Portugal meant that seaports sprung up early. Today, the most important ports are Lisbon, Porto, Setúbal, and Sines. The three major airports on the continent are in Lisbon, Faro, and Porto.

The islands in the Atlantic also have up-to-date transportation. The seaports in Funchal and Ponta Delgada are important links between the Madeira and

ABOVE: *Aerial view of Lisbon's port, where shipping containers are loaded and unloaded.*

EUROPEAN COUNTRIES TODAY: PORTUGAL

The Economy of Portugal

Gross Domestic Product (GDP): $298.6 billion (2016 est.)
GDP Per Capita: $28,900 (2016 est.)
Industries: textiles, clothing, footwear, wood and cork, paper and pulp, chemicals, fuels and lubricants, automobiles and auto parts, base metals, minerals, porcelain and ceramics, glassware, technology, telecommunications; dairy products, wine, other foodstuffs; ship construction and refurbishment; tourism, plastics, financial services, optics
Agriculture: potatoes, fruits, vegetables, wheat; poultry, eggs, pork, dairy
Export Commodities: agricultural products, foodstuffs, wine, oil products, chemical products, plastics and rubber, hides, leather, wood and cork, wood pulp and paper, textile materials, clothing, footwear, machinery and tools, base metals
Export Partners: Spain 26.2%, France 12.6%, Germany 11.7%, UK 7%, US 4.9% (2016)
Import Commodities: agricultural products, chemical products, vehicles and other transport material, optical and precision instruments, computer accessories and parts, semiconductors and related devices, oil products, base metals, food products, textile materials
Import Partners: Spain 32.8%, Germany 13.5%, France 7.8%, Italy 5.5%, Netherlands 5.1% (2016)
Currency: euro

Source: www.cia.gov 2017

THE PORTUGUESE ECONOMY

Azores islands and the rest of the world. Airports in Funchal, Porto Santo, and Ponta Delgada also bring people to and from the islands.

A Recovering Economy

After the recession of 2008 to 2009, Portugal's economy began to grow again, but only very slightly and recovery was fragile. To help Portugal, in 2011, the EU and IMF finalized a rescue package. By 2014, Portugal had exited the EU and IMF rescue package as its economy started to gather steam. The Portuguese government managed to reverse some of the more unpopular austerity measures but remained within most of the EU fiscal targets. The budget deficit fell from 11 percent of GDP in 2010 to 2 percent in 2016, the country's lowest since 1974, and surpassed the EU and IMF projections.

ABOVE: *Portugal is endowed with a sunny climate and a beautiful coastline. It has many stunning beaches, making it a perfect destination for a vacation.*

EUROPEAN COUNTRIES TODAY: PORTUGAL

Tourism

Situated in the southwest of Europe, just a few hours from other European capitals, Portugal is a magnet for tourists. There is no doubt that Portugal is an extremely beautiful country with a lot to offer, including stunning scenery, interesting historic and religious sites, and wonderful beaches. The country also has a favorable climate suitable for a wide range of visitors. Tourism in Portugal not only serves international visitors but also the Portuguese, who spend many vacations on Portuguese soil. Every year, the country attracts millions of tourists, the most popular destinations being Lisbon, northern Portugal, and the Algarve for international travelers. National tourists, however, prefer northern Portugal, followed by central Portugal and Lisbon.

Text-Dependent Questions

1. What are the main crops grown in Portugal?

2. What are the most important ports in Portugal?

3. Why is Portugal a popular tourist destination?

Research Project

Write an essay about tourism in Portugal. Compare and contrast the different destinations that tourists can visit.

Words to Understand

diversity: The state of having people who are of different races or who have different cultures in a group or organization.

homogeneous: Of the same or a similar kind or nature.

troubadours: Writers and performers of songs or poetry in the Middle Ages.

BELOW: Residential houses in the Bairro Alto district of Lisbon.

Chapter Four
CITIZENS OF PORTUGAL: PEOPLE, CUSTOMS & CULTURE

Portugal tends to have a **homogeneous** population, although the cities are more ethnically diverse. Most Portuguese are descended from the Celtiberians; this group mixed with the Romans and Visigoths who later invaded the area. Only about 4 percent of the population today is made up of immigrants, most of whom are Ukrainians, Brazilians, Cape Verdeans, and Angolans. The lack of **diversity** means that most Portuguese people have strong ties, socially and historically, to each other; this has created a rich and interesting culture in Portugal.

ABOVE: The food hall in the Mercado da Ribeira at Cais do Sodré is near the train station in Lisbon. There are thirty-two restaurants in the complex offering many types of cuisine.

CITIZENS OF PORTUGAL: PEOPLE, CUSTOMS & CULTURE

ABOVE: The Queima das Fitas *(Burning of the Ribbons) parade is a traditional festival attended by students from Portuguese universities, celebrating graduation.*

EUROPEAN COUNTRIES TODAY: PORTUGAL

Educational Video

A guide to Portugal's heritage.

The Portuguese Language

Spoken by more than 250 million people, Portuguese is the third-most spoken European language in the world, following English and Spanish. This is a striking reminder of the Portuguese empire left in its former colonies, in places like Brazil, Angola, Cape Verde, and East Timor.

In Portugal, the overwhelming majority of people speak Portuguese, which is the official language. Many people have been taught Spanish, English, and French, and can speak them fluently, as in many other European countries.

Education

Education in Portugal has improved greatly in recent years. Portugal's government has invested in education, which has led to better opportunities for all of its citizens. This has helped the economy by supplying a pool of better educated workers. Despite these improvements, however, the literacy rate in Portugal is still lower than in some other EU countries, but it is improving.

The current education system is divided into *pré-escolar*, which is attended by children younger than six; the *ensino básico*, which children go to for nine years; *ensino secundário*, a three-year level; and *ensino superior*, made up of universities and polytechnic schools. School is free and compulsory for nine years, but more and more people are attending further education institutions.

An improved education system has brought about improvements to all aspects of life, including job quality, health care, housing, and society in general.

CITIZENS OF PORTUGAL: PEOPLE, CUSTOMS & CULTURE

ABOVE: Grilled sardines are very popular in Portugal and are usually served with wedges of lemons.

Feijão à Portuguesa

Food

The country's close proximity to the sea means that fish and shellfish are a major part of the Portuguese diet. Cod is one of the most widely used fish and is often made into codfish cakes or grilled. Popular foods include grilled sardines (*sardinhas asadas*), tuna steak (*bife de atum*). Menus also contain other food grown on Portuguese land, especially potatoes. Perhaps one of the foods most identified with Portugal's cuisine is a custard tart known as a *pastiés de nata*.

Portuguese wines (*vinhos*) are world famous and are enjoyed with meals. Strong coffee is also popular, particularly with dessert.

Feijão à Portuguesa
(Portuguese Bean Stew)

Makes about 6–8 servings

Ingredients
1 pound dried navy beans
Water as needed
1 large onion, chopped
1 red bell pepper, sliced
3 garlic cloves, minced
1 6-ounce can tomato paste
1 pound Spanish chorizo, cut into ¼-inch slices
½ teaspoon dried red pepper flakes
1 teaspoon sweet paprika

EUROPEAN COUNTRIES TODAY: PORTUGAL

1 tablespoon olive oil
salt and pepper to taste

Directions
Wash beans and soak overnight in enough cold water to cover by several inches. Before using the next day, drain and rinse the beans and set aside. In a skillet add the olive oil and fry the onion and bell pepper until soft, about 8 minutes. Add the garlic and cook for 1 minute. Add beans, 8 cups of water, tomato paste, chorizo, red pepper flakes, and paprika. Cover and simmer until the beans are tender, 1 ½ to 2 hours, stirring occasionally to prevent scorching.

Broa Doce

Broa Doce (Sweet Bread)

Ingredients
¼ cup butter or margarine, melted
¾ cup 1% milk
⅓ cup granulated sugar
1 packet active dry yeast
2 eggs, room temperature
3–3¼ cups flour
⅓ teaspoon salt
1 egg yolk
2 tablespoons water
1 tablespoon coarse or raw sugar

Directions
Melt butter in saucepan on stovetop. Add milk and sugar; stir well and heat to 110°F, slightly more than lukewarm. Pour into a mixing bowl, stir in yeast to dissolve, and let stand 10 minutes. Beat in eggs, then gradually beat in flour and salt. On a slightly floured surface, knead dough until smooth and elastic. Cover with a damp towel and let rise until doubled.

Punch down the dough, shape into a 7-inch round. Place in greased 9-inch cake pan. Beat egg yolk with water and brush over dough; sprinkle with raw sugar. Cover with damp towel and let rise in a warm place until doubled. Preheat oven to 350°F. Bake 45 to 50 minutes, or until well browned and hollow sounding when tapped lightly. Cool on rack. Serve warm or toasted. To serve, cut into quarters then slice each quarter into five slices, each about 1 inch thick.

CITIZENS OF PORTUGAL: PEOPLE, CUSTOMS & CULTURE

Literature Though the Ages

Portugal's literature took off during the thirteenth and fourteenth centuries, when **troubadours**, traveling musicians, and poets spread knowledge throughout the area. In the 1500s, poet Luís de Camões and dramatist Gil Vicente wrote and published several works. De Camões, who wrote the epic *The Lusiads*, is celebrated as a national cultural hero today.

Portugal boasts several modern-day writers who have achieved fame. Modern literature includes several poets, including Frenando Pessoa, who wrote during the early 1900s, and writer José Saramago, who won the Nobel Prize for Literature in 1998.

The Arts: Music and Architecture

Portugal lays claim to the *fado*, a local form of music unique to the country and often described as sad and melancholy. The songs, of which there are thousands, are said to have come from the music of sailors during the sixteenth century, African slave songs, and Arabic music. Folk dancing sometimes accompanies these fados.

Other types of music are popular as well. Hip Hop Tuga, a type of music that is a mix of pop, African music, and reggae, is listened to by the younger generation.

The architecture that can be found in Portugal's cities, as well as its countryside, is often stunning. The Romans, the Moors, and

ABOVE: *Luís de Camões.*

ABOVE: *Frenando Pessoa.*

ABOVE: *José Saramago.*

today's modernism all influenced the country's buildings. Portugal is also home to one of the best schools for architecture in the world, the Escola do Porto.

Religion

Most of Portugal's people are Roman Catholic. Almost 85 percent say they belong to this faith. Protestants make up the largest religious minority, followed by Muslims and Hindus. There is also a tiny number of Jews living in the country.

ABOVE: *Teens performing a traditional Portuguese folk dance at a folklore festival in Mértola, in the southeast of Portugal, near the Spanish border.*

Palaces of Sintra

The attractive little town of Sintra is set among the hilly woodlands of the Sierra de Sintra, about fifteen miles west of Lisbon. Its charms were celebrated by the great Portuguese national poet Luís de Camões, and later by Lord Byron in *Childe Harold's Pilgrimage*. For centuries it was the summer refuge of the Portuguese royal family. Among their memorials are the royal palace in the Old Town, partly wrecked in the earthquake of 1755 but afterwards restored, and the spectacular Palacio da Pena, which crowns a hilltop.

The royal palace (inset), brusquely described by one writer as Moorish and debased Gothic, and by an eighteenth-century English visitor as "this confused pile," is not a prepossessing building from the outside. The first one is likely to see of it is the enormous conical chimneys of the kitchens. It was once thought to be an old Moorish palace, but it seems to have been built from scratch in the reign of João I (1385–1433), though with many Moorish characteristics and on the site of a Muslim building. It has also many features of the curious Portuguese late-Gothic style known as Manueline, which itself owed something to Iberian Islamic tradition.

The extraordinary Gothic Palacio da Pena (left) incorporates the Monastery of Our Lady of Pena, which was built about 1500. The monastic ruins were bought in 1839 by Ferdinand of Saxe-Coburg-Gotha (first cousin of both Queen Victoria and Prince Albert), who had married Maria II of Portugal in 1836, receiving the title of king-consort. With the advice of a Prussian engineer, Ludwig von Eschwege, he greatly enlarged it and turned it into a Romantic medieval palace, part monastery, part castle, as a gift for his wife. Opinion on such a building is bound to be highly subjective, but Ferdinand's project, judged on his terms, is a dramatic success. The intensely Romantic atmosphere is heightened by the richly exotic furnishings and, in the chapel, a fine Renaissance altar piece. Today, the palace is the scene of concerts and other cultural activities.

CITIZENS OF PORTUGAL: PEOPLE, CUSTOMS & CULTURE

ABOVE: *Guarda Cathedral was founded in 1390 and completed in 1540. The town of Guarda is Portugal's highest town and situated in the Serra da Estrela mountains.*

Despite this lack of religious diversity, Portugal's constitution guarantees its citizens the right to the freedom of religion.

Sports

As in other European countries, the most popular sport in Portugal is soccer (or football, as it's known in Europe). The Portuguese love to play as much as watch. Portugal has an excellent national team, ranked third in the world in 2017, and the city of Porto's team has won several cup titles.

Portugal also has a type of national martial arts, called *Jogo do pau*, or Portuguese stick combat, since it involves wooden sticks as weapons. The sport originated during medieval times and was used as a style of dueling between young men fighting over a woman. Today, it is a way to celebrate the Portuguese national heritage.

EUROPEAN COUNTRIES TODAY: PORTUGAL

ABOVE: *The Festa dos Tabuleiros (Festival of the Trays) or Festa do Divino Espírito Santo (Feast of the Holy Spirit), takes place every four years in June or July in Tomar. The festival is an ancient tradition that attracts people from all over the world.*

CITIZENS OF PORTUGAL: PEOPLE, CUSTOMS & CULTURE

ABOVE: *Cristiano Ronaldo is a Portuguese professional footballer who plays as a forward for Spanish club Real Madrid and the Portuguese national team. Ronaldo is considered by many to be the best player in the world at this current time.*

EUROPEAN COUNTRIES TODAY: PORTUGAL

ABOVE: Portugal (in green) vs. Hungary, in a qualifier for the World Cup that was held in Russia in 2018.

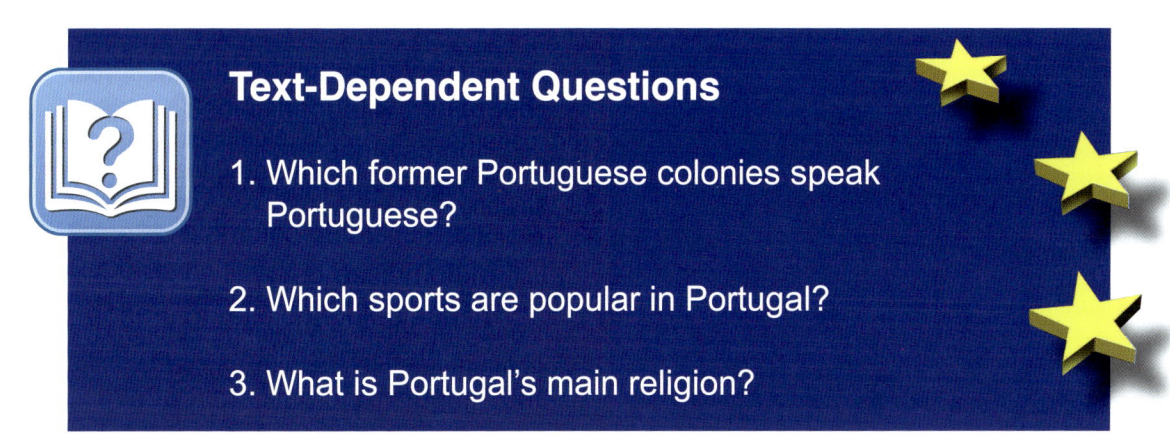

Text-Dependent Questions

1. Which former Portuguese colonies speak Portuguese?

2. Which sports are popular in Portugal?

3. What is Portugal's main religion?

Research Project

Write a one-page biography on Luís de Camões.

Words to Understand

colonies: Distant territories belonging to or under the control of a nation.

emancipated: To be freed from someone else's control or power.

urban: Relating to cities and the people who live in them.

BELOW: The sixteenth-century Belém Tower, or the Tower of St. Vincent, is a fortified tower located in the civil parish of Santa Maria de Belém, Lisbon. It is a World Heritage Site.

Chapter Five
THE FAMOUS CITIES OF PORTUGAL

Portugal's cities reflect its long history, as well as the progress the country has made in recent years. A significant portion of the people who live in Portugal are former inhabitants of the colonies Portugal emancipated in 1994. Seven percent of the total population is made up of people from places such as the former Portuguese colonies in Africa.

Approximately one-third of the population lives in urban and suburban areas around Lisbon, the capital, and Porto. This reflects the continuing movement of people from rural farming communities to more commercial areas, showing the rising importance of Portugal's cities.

Lisbon

Lisbon, or Lisboa in Portuguese, has been Portugal's capital since 1255. As the capital, Lisbon is the center of the government as well as of the culture. The city is home to many cafés, restaurants, and shopping opportunities. It also has over fifty museums; three universities; stunning architecture, such as the

ABOVE: The Monument of the Discoveries, Belém, Lisbon. The monument celebrates the Portuguese age of exploration during the fifteenth and sixteenth centuries.

THE FAMOUS CITIES OF PORTUGAL

Educational Video

A travel guide to Portugal's capital city, Lisbon.

ABOVE: St. Georges Castle in Lisbon stands majestically above the town. The castle was the ancient seat of power for Portugal for over four hundred years.

EUROPEAN COUNTRIES TODAY: PORTUGAL

ABOVE: *The streetcars in Lisbon are not only great for getting around the city but are also one of Lisbon's most important tourist attractions.*

Belém and St. George's Castle; and historic yellow electric tramcars. The Baixa, or lower town, is an important cultural and historical area of the city.

Its location on the Tagus River gives Lisbon a water trade route, but also a picturesque background. Water sports are popular pastimes, as is strolling along the green banks of the river.

Royal Palace, Queluz

The Palace of Queluz, which is in the district of Lisbon on the road to Sintra, was begun in 1747, and much of it was completed by 1752. This attractive rococo residence, one of the few royal palaces one would like to live in, was designed for a younger son of the Portuguese royal family and was financed out of the profits of the gold and diamonds produced by Brazil. Although not finished at the time of the great Lisbon earthquake of 1755, it suffered comparatively little. It was badly damaged by fire in the 1930s but subsequently restored.

The palace itself, set amid flower gardens, is the masterpiece of a Portuguese architect, Mateus Vicente de Oliveira (1710–60), and has an unpretentious charm and a sense of easy assurance. Among the main rooms is the Sala das Mangas, with panels of *azulejos* (decorative tiles) in the "Chinese" manner covering most of the walls, predominantly in blue and gold. The Hall of

Mirrors glitters with glass and gilt. In the Ball Room, also with shimmering chandeliers, the rococo decoration is most lavish, and the room is planned on an elliptical oval.

Other architects and designers, including a Frenchman, Jean-Baptiste Robillon, were engaged on other buildings and features of the gardens that augment Oliveira's perfectly proportioned central block. Robillon planned the hanging gardens; the extensive topiary was the work of a Dutchman, Gerald van der Kolk, and the lead statues, a fashion also stemming from the Netherlands, were by an Englishman, John Cheeve. The extraordinary little western pavilion, reached by the dramatic Lion's Steps, is by Robillon. From a staid classical colonnade, Rococo statuary breaks into a riot against the sky. The eastern pavilion, with its scrolled pediments, is also interesting, but its designer is unknown.

THE FAMOUS CITIES OF PORTUGAL

ABOVE: *The famous arch at the entrance to the Praça do Comércio, a square in Lisbon, next to the Tagus River.*

EUROPEAN COUNTRIES TODAY: PORTUGAL

ABOVE: The Church of Santa Engrácia in Lisbon was built in the seventeenth century. Originally a church, it was converted into the National Pantheon in the twentieth century. It is a site where many important Portuguese have been buried.

THE FAMOUS CITIES OF PORTUGAL

Vasco da Gama Bridge

The Vasco da Gama Bridge is the longest bridge in Europe. It measures over 10 miles (17 km) long and connects the northern regions with the southern regions of Portugal. The bridge is a modern cable-stayed bridge that spans the estuary of the Tagus River. It was opened to traffic in 1998, in time for the Lisbon World Exposition. On cloudy days, it is impossible to see the other side of the bridge, it is so long!

The bridge was named after Portuguese discoverer, Vasco da Gama, and its opening commemorated the fifth centenary of his arrival from India in 1498. Da Gama was the first European to reach India by sea, via the Atlantic Ocean. The Vasco da Gama Bridge was designed by Armando Rito Engineering, a company that specializes in the design of large-scale bridges and viaducts.

EUROPEAN COUNTRIES TODAY: PORTUGAL

Porto

Porto is northern Portugal's largest city and the country's second-largest city. The city, which has been made famous by the wine sharing its name, is classified as a World Heritage Site, demonstrating its importance. Much of the city dates back to medieval times, or even to the period of Roman rule.

ABOVE: *Porto is situated on the Douro River estuary in northern Portugal. Porto is the country's second-largest city.*

THE FAMOUS CITIES OF PORTUGAL

ABOVE: Porto Cathedral is a Roman Catholic church located in the historical center of the city of Porto. It is one of the city's oldest monuments and one of the most important local Romanesque buildings.

EUROPEAN COUNTRIES TODAY: PORTUGAL

In 2001, Porto was declared to be one of the European Culture Capitals. This brought more prosperity to the region, as well as a concert hall called Casa da Música. Porto is also home to the Fantasporto International Film Festival.

ABOVE: *The historical center of Porto is home to narrow, winding streets.*

THE FAMOUS CITIES OF PORTUGAL

Coimbra

Coimbra is another of Portugal's large cities, located between Lisbon and Porto, in the center of Portugal. It is ranked third in importance after these two cities. Like them, Coimbra is a center for culture and history, as well as shopping and dining. Museums, libraries, parks, and monuments attract both locals and tourists.

ABOVE: *The old town of Coimbra. The university at the top of the hill is in the background.*

EUROPEAN COUNTRIES TODAY: PORTUGAL

ABOVE: The Santa Cruz Monastery (Monastery of the Holy Cross) is a National Monument in Coimbra.

THE FAMOUS CITIES OF PORTUGAL

During the twelfth and thirteen centuries, Coimbra was Portugal's capital. Today, it is more famous as home to the University of Coimbra, the seventh-oldest university in Europe. The university contains interesting architecture, as does the rest of the city. Because the city is so old, Roman ruins can be found at the city's archeological site.

ABOVE: The central square of Coimbra is a favorite destination for tourists to visit.

EUROPEAN COUNTRIES TODAY: PORTUGAL

ABOVE: Praça Luís de Camões is a beautiful square in the popular seaside town of Lagos, on the Algarve.

Lagos

Located on the coast of the Algarve, Lagos attracts many tourists. The beaches are breathtaking and the weather is consistently warm. Tourists and locals alike can enjoy the sun and the outdoors by renting mopeds or taking boat trips from the harbor. Culturally, Lagos is known for the Museu Municipal, a fascinating museum that contains unusual exhibits.

THE FAMOUS CITIES OF PORTUGAL

ABOVE: *Fishing and rowing boats in the harbor at Setúbal.*

EUROPEAN COUNTRIES TODAY: PORTUGAL

Setúbal

The city of Setúbal is located on the mouth of the Sado River, approximately 30 miles (48 km) south of Portugal's capital, Lisbon. Setúbal has a long and very interesting history dating back to Roman times. The city has always had a strong relationship with the sea, and it is said that it was founded by a relative of Noah. It has a fishing industry dating back two thousand years. Today, Setúbal is famous for its hundreds of colored fishing boats tied up along the riverfront. This picturesque scene has become a haven for tourists and the city now has excellent hotels, resorts, and the infrastructure required for a bustling tourist destination. In the downtown area, there are many interesting shops to visit, including those selling traditional crafts as well as global brands. The key meeting place in Setúbal is the Praça do Bocage, where the people of the city converge to socialize.

Text-Dependent Questions

1. How long has Lisbon been Portugal's capital city?

2. Where is the city of Porto located?

3. Why is Lagos particularly attractive to tourists?

Research Project

Choose a Portuguese town or city not mentioned in this chapter and write a short essay about its history, culture, and location.

Words to Understand

fossil fuels: Fuels (such as coal, oil, or natural gas) formed in the earth from plant or animal remains.

investment: The act of committing money in order to gain a profit.

renewable energy: Any naturally occurring, inexhaustible source of energy (e.g., biomass, solar, wind, tidal, wave, and hydroelectric power), that is not derived from fossil or nuclear fuel.

BELOW: The beautiful coast of the Algarve is very popular with tourists. Tourism is an important part of Portugal's future.

Chapter Six
A BRIGHT FUTURE FOR PORTUGAL

Portugal has not always had things easy, and in recent years the country has suffered from a struggling economy. But as it moves toward the future, it has started to find ways of addressing its financial problems and is now finding its way out of a difficult situation. However, when it comes to **investment** for the future, Portugal is way ahead of much of the rest of the world.

Renewable Energy

Portugal's leaders have made a commitment to reduce their nation's dependence on **fossil fuels**. In 2005, they began an ambitious program to harness the country's wind, rivers, sunlight, and ocean waves. By 2016, nearly 95 percent of all Portugal's domestic electricity came from **renewable energy** sources. The country has also planned to put into use a national network of charging stations for electric cars. Portugal is now on track to reach its goal of using only renewable energy for domestic purposes by 2020.

The Portuguese, however, pay nearly twice as much as Americans do for their electricity. (But the United States gets less than 15

ABOVE: *Portuguese and EU flags.*

A BRIGHT FUTURE FOR PORTUGAL

ABOVE: *Pomarão dam and hydroelectric power station on the Chança Reservoir near the Guadiana River, which is on the border between Portugal and Spain.*

percent of its energy from renewable sources.) With Portugal facing such serious economic problems, its energy policy is becoming increasingly controversial. But Portugal's leaders are convinced that renewable energy is worth the cost.

And even though Portugal's energy costs are greater than in the United States, they're about average for the rest of Europe. Portugal has done a good job at keeping costs down as much as possible by focusing on the cheapest forms of renewable energy—wind and hydropower—while giving incentives to private companies to build renewable power plants. The government has stated that the total investment in rebuilding Portugal's energy structure will be very costly, but that this cost will be borne by private companies. One considerable advantage for the future is that Portugal will be able to export electricity to Spain.

EUROPEAN COUNTRIES TODAY: PORTUGAL

ABOVE: Wind turbines on the hills in central Portugal.

A BRIGHT FUTURE FOR PORTUGAL

The electricity that comes from natural forces like wind and water can be unpredictable though. A wind farm that produces 200 megawatts of electricity one hour may produce only 5 megawatts a few hours later when the wind dies down. Solar panels may not do so well on cloudy days, and hydropower may be plentiful during a rainy winter but not during a dry summer. Meanwhile, people's energy needs are fairly constant.

But Portugal's energy program has found ways to deal with this problem. It has experts who predict the weather, especially wind patterns. They route energy from one part of the grid to another as needed. The program requires a good amount of coordination, expertise, and organization in real-time situations.

ABOVE: *Solar panels make the most of Portugal's high levels of sunshine.*

EUROPEAN COUNTRIES TODAY: PORTUGAL

What Is Global Climate Change—and Why Are People So Worried About It?

Global climate change has to do with an average increase in the Earth's temperature. Most scientists agree that humans are responsible because of the pollution that cars and factories have put into the air.

Global warming is already having serious impacts on humans and the environment in many ways. An increase in global temperatures causes rising sea levels (because of melting of the polar caps) and changes in the amount and pattern of precipitation. These changes may increase the frequency and intensity of extreme weather events, such as floods, droughts, heat waves, hurricanes, and tornados. Other consequences include changes to farms' crop production, species becoming extinct, and an increased spread of disease.

Not all experts agree about climate change, but almost all scientists believe that it is very real. Politicians and the public do not agree, though, on policies to deal with climate change. Changes in the way people live can be expensive, at both the personal and national levels, and not everyone is convinced that taking on these expenses needs to be a priority.

There are decisions to be made—every hour, every second. The objective is to keep the system alive and avoid blackouts.

Portugal's program also combines wind and water. Wind-driven turbines pump water uphill at night, when winds tend to be stronger, and then the water flows downhill by day, generating electricity when consumer demand is highest.

85

A BRIGHT FUTURE FOR PORTUGAL

Portugal's distribution system doesn't just deliver electricity either; it also draws electricity from even the smallest generators, like rooftop solar panels. The government works hard to encourage people to install these rooftop panels.

Portugal, like the EU as a whole, believes that one of the biggest challenges facing the entire world is global climate change. The economy of every nation in the world depends on the health of our planet in order to thrive. The greater the number of nations switching to clean energy sources, the smaller the amount of greenhouse gases being emitted—and the safer our future will be.

Dangerous Drugs

In 2001, newspapers around the world carried graphic reports of Portugal's heroin addicts, calling the slums of Lisbon (Portugal's capital city) Europe's "most shameful neighborhood" and its "worst drugs ghetto." So in the same year, the world was shocked by a decision the Portuguese government had made: to decriminalize the personal use and possession of all drugs, including heroin and cocaine. In other words, using drugs is no longer a serious crime in Portugal. The Portuguese police were told not to arrest anyone found taking any kind of drug.

Despite condemnation from around the world, Portugal now has one of Europe's lowest lifetime usage rates for marijuana. Heroin and other drug abuse has decreased among teenagers, and the percentage of heroin users who inject the drug has also fallen, from 45 percent before decriminalization to 17 percent now. Drug addicts now account for only 20 percent of Portugal's HIV cases, down from 56 percent before the new drug policy.

Now the world is paying attention to Portugal's drug policy, looking for answers to the drug problems the entire world faces. Drug rehabilitation organizations have realized that solutions for the future may lie in Portugal.

Hope for the Future

Portugal's innovative and aggressive approaches to energy and drugs prove that this nation has the ability to find its own unique solutions to tough problems that the entire world faces. Now it needs to put that same innovative and

EUROPEAN COUNTRIES TODAY: PORTUGAL

aggressive spirit to work on the other problems that are holding this nation back as it moves into the twenty-first century. If Portugal can do that, with support from the EU, this nation could turn its future around completely, creating better days ahead for the Portuguese people.

Future Challenges

Portugal's public debt: The Portuguese national debt is around 132 percent of the GDP as of 2017. This problem is a threat to the Portuguese economy and the state's financial sustainability.

ABOVE: The decriminalization of drugs in Portugal has led to a large decrease in the number of addicts in the country.

A BRIGHT FUTURE FOR PORTUGAL

Forest fires: Like other countries with very hot summers, every year large areas of Portuguese forest are destroyed.

A large public sector: The public sector is a very large, expensive, and inefficient part of the Portuguese economy. An excess of public employees and bureaucracy results in very high costs for the taxpayer.

ABOVE: *Approaching the Port of Leixões, near Porto. Portugal's infrastructure has benefited from EU funding nationwide.*

EUROPEAN COUNTRIES TODAY: PORTUGAL

Portugal and the EU

Since joining the EU in 1986, Portugal has come a long way. Today, itl has become one of the leading powers of the EU. The country has held the presidency of the EU three times, most recently in 2007. Today, Portugal is a fully functioning member of the EU. It has twenty-one seats in the EU Parliament and twelve votes in the Council. Portugal also contributes nearly 1.5 billion euros to the EU's budget.

From its rich history, to its fascinating cities, to its interesting people, Portugal is poised to help bring peace and prosperity to the EU, as well as to itself. Its future looks hopeful for both its people and its economy as it begins to work more closely with its neighboring European countries.

Text-Dependent Questions

1. What kinds of renewable energy does Portugal generate?

2. Why are drug laws in Portugal controversial?

3. How much does Portugal pay into the EU per year?

Research Project

Learn Portuguese expressions for simple words such as hello, good day, please, and thank you. Try them on your friends.

CHRONOLOGY

5500 BCE	Fortified villages are established in the Tagus Valley.
700	Celts arrive on the Iberian Peninsula.
219	Romans invade the Iberian Peninsula.
c. 400	Visigoths take over Iberia.
711 CE	Moors invade Portugal, and the Golden Age begins.
c.1000	Christians drive Moors from peninsula; Christian reconquest of the peninsula begins.
1143	Portugal is officially recognized as a country.
1400s	Portugal enters age of expansion.
1539	Court of Inquisition set up.
1580	Spain annexes Portugal.
1640	Portugal regains its independence from Spain.
1822	Constitutional monarchy is created.
1828	King Miguel I declares the constitution null.
1916	Portugal enters World War I.
1926	The military takes over the government, and Salazar becomes dictator.
1939	World War II starts.
1955	Portugal is admitted to the United Nations.
1986	Portugal becomes a member of the European Economic Community.
1999	Portugal joins the European Monetary Union.
2001	Portugal decriminalizes drug use.
2002	Portugal begins to use the euro as its currency.
2005	Portugal begins a clean energy program and totally revamps its energy production.
2011	The government announces the country's biggest spending cuts in fifty years.
2015	António Costa forms centre-left government.
2016	Former prime minister António Guterres is appointed UN secretary general.
2017	Portugal drops complaint to the EU over Spain's plan to build a nuclear waste storage facility that environmentalists fear could affect the River Tagus, which flows into Portugal.

Further Reading

McCormick, John. *Understanding the European Union: A Concise Introduction.* London: Palgrave Macmillan, 2017.

Mason, David S. *A Concise History of Modern Europe: Liberty, Equality, Solidarity.* London: Rowman & Littlefield, 2015.

St. Louis, Regis. Armstrong, Kate. Christiani, Kerry. Di Duca, Marc. Mutic, Anja. Raub, Kevin. *Lonely Planet Portugal (Travel Guide).* London: Lonely Planet Publications, 2017.

Steves, Rick. *Rick Steves Portugal.* Edmonds: Rick Steves' Europe, Inc. 2017.

Internet Resources

Portugal Travel Information and Travel Guide
www.lonelyplanet.com/portugal

Portugal Travel Website
https://www.visitportugal.com

Portugal: Country Profile
http://www.bbc.co.uk/news/world-europe-17758217

Portugal: CIA World Factbook
https://www.cia.gov/library/publications/the-world-factbook/geos/po.html

The Official Website of the European Union
europa.eu/index_en.htm

Publisher's note:
The websites listed on this page were active at the time of publication. The publisher is not responsible for websites that have changed their addresses or discontinued operation since the date of publication. The publisher will review and update the website list upon each reprint.

INDEX

A

AD (anno Domini), 26
Afonso Henriques, 27
Africa, 15, 29, 30, 34, 63
Agriculture, 38, 40, 41, 42, 45
Airports, 44, 46
Albert, Prince, 57
Alentejo, 14, 41
Alfonso I, 8
Algarve, 12, 14, 16, 17, 25, 28, 40, 47, 77, 80
Allies, 32
Alqueva reservoir, 20
Andalus, al-, 25
Angola, 51
Angolans, 49
Animals, 18, 19, 20
Architecture, 54–55
    Manueline, 57
    modernism, 55
    Romanesque, 72
    Romantic, 57
Area, 7, 11
Armando Rito Engineering, 70
Arts, 27, 54–55
Assembly of the Republic, 35
Astúrias-León, 27
Atlantic Ocean, 7, 12, 14, 70
Azores Islands, 7, 12, 13, 14, 15, 19, 46
Azulejos (decorative tiles), 66

B

Bairro Alto, 48
Baixa, 65
Battle of Ourique, 8
BC (Before Christ), 26
BCE (Before Common Era), 26
Beaches, 46, 47, 77
Belém, 63, 65
    Tower (Tower of St. Vincent), 62

Belgium, 37
Berlengas archipelago, 11
Birth rate, 9
Borders, 7
Brazil, 29, 51, 66
Brazilians, 49
Bridge, 70
Broa Doce, 52–53
Brussels, 36
Byron, Lord, 56

C

Caetano, Marcello, 34
Cais do Sodré, 49
Camões, Luis de, 54, 56
Cape Verde, 51
Cape Verdeans, 49
Capital, 63, 76, 85
Casa da Música, 73
Castle of the Moors, 24
CE (Common Era), 26
Celtiberians, 49
Celts, 23
Chamber of Deputies, 31
Chança Reservoir, 82
Cheeve, John, 67
Childe Harolds' Pilgrimage (Byron), 56
Church of Santa Engrácia, 69
Circumnavigation, 8
Cities, 63–79
Citrus fruit, 40
Climate, 7, 17, 47
Coasts, 17, 19, 46
Coimbra, 74–76
Colonies, 34, 51, 63
Constitution, 31–32
Constitutional Charter, 32
Cork, 42, 43
Costa, António, 34, 35
Council of Ministers, 35
County of Portugal, 27

Court
    of Inquisition, 29
    system, 31, 35
Culture, 49–61
Currency, 37, 39, 45

D

Dating systems, 26
Death rate, 9
Decline, 30
Deforestation, 21
Democracy, 31, 34
    overthrow of, 32
Dictatorship, 32, 33
Diversity, 49
Douro
    River, 17, 26, 71
    Valley, 38
Drugs, 86
    decriminalization, 85, 87

E

Early Portugal, 23
East Timor, 51
Economy, 34, 35, 39–47, 51
    austerity, 35, 46
    diversification, 39
    projections, 39
    public debt, 87
    public sector, 88
    recovery, 46
    rescue package, 46
Education, 27, 51
    ensino básico, 51
    ensino secundário, 51
    ensino superior, 51
    pré-escolar, 51
Electricity, 81, 84, 85, 86
Elevations, 7
Empire, 11, 30–31
Energy

INDEX

costs, 82
renewable, 81–86
English language, 51
Environment, 20–21
Eschwege, Ludwig von, 57
Escola do Porto, 55
Ethnic groups, 9, 49
Euro, 37, 39, 45
European
    Coal and Steel Community, 37
    Community, 34, 37, 39
    Council, 36, 89
    Culture Capitals, 73
    Economic Community, 37
    Monetary Union, 34
European Union (EU), 34, 46, 89
    autonomy, 36
    budget, 89
    flag, 81
    formation, 36–37
    member, 36, 37
    Parliament, 89
    Parliament Building, 36
    presidency, 89
    single market, 37
    values, 36
Eurozone, 39
Évora, 41
Exploration, 29, 63, 70
Exports, 42, 45

F

Fado, 54
Fantasporto International Film Festival, 73
Faro, 44
Feijão à Portuguesa, 52–53
Felipe I, 30
Ferdinand of Saxe-Coburg-Gotha, 57

Festa
    do Divino Espírto Santo (Feast of the Holy Spirit), 59
    dos Tabuleiros (Festival of the Trays), 59
Fish, 52
Fishing, 39, 41, 78
Flag, 8, 81
Flora and fauna, 19–20
Folk dance, 55
Food, 52–53
Football, 58, 60, 61
Forest, 19–20
    fires, 88
Formation, 27
Fort of São João Baptista das Berlengas, 11
Fossil fuels, 81
France, 36, 37, 42, 45
French
    language, 51
    Revolution, 31
Funchal, 44, 46
Future, 81–89

G

Gama, Vasco da, 70
Geography, 7
    and landscape, 11–22
Germany, 42, 45
Global
    climate change, 85, 86
    warming, 85
Government, 23–37
Grapes, 38
Greeks, 23
Grilled sardines *(sardinhas asadas)*, 52
Gross domestic product (GDP), 41, 45, 46, 87
    per capita, 45

Guadiana River, 20
Guarda, 58
    Cathedral, 58
Guimarães, 27

H

Hazards, 7
Henry the Navigator, Prince, 29
Heresy, 29
Heroin, 85
Hinduism, 55
Hip Hop Tuga, 54
History, 23–37
Hungary, 61

I

Iberia, 23
Iberian
    lynx, 19
    Peninsula, 8, 11
    wolf, 18
Ilha do Pico, 7
Immigrants, 49
Imports, 42, 45
Independence, 30
India, 29, 70
Industry, 42, 45
Infant mortality rate, 9
Inhabitation, 23
Inquisition, 29
International Monetary Fund, 35, 46
Islam, 9, 23, 27, 55
Islands, 13, 14, 44
Italy, 37, 42, 45

J

João
    I, 28, 29, 57
    III, 29, 30

INDEX

Jogo do pau, 58
Judaism, 9, 29, 55

K
Kolk, Gerald van der, 67

L
Lagoa, 16
    Comprida, 13
    das Sete Cidades, 15
Lagos, 77
Lakes, 13, 15
Language, 9, 51
Life expectancy, 9
Lisboa, 85. *See* Lisbon
Lisbon, 8, 13, 17, 44, 47, 48, 49, 62, 63–69, 74, 79
    World Exposition, 70
Literacy rate, 9, 51
Literature, 54
Lusiads, The (Camões), 54
Lusitanians, 23
Luxembourg, 37

M
Maastricht Treaty, 37
Madeira Islands, 13, 14, 15, 19, 44
Map, 6, 30–31
Maria II, 57
Marijuana, 85
Mercado da Ribeira, 49
Merger Treaty, 37
Mértola, 55
Metro, 44
Migration rate, 9
Miguel I, 32
Mining, 42
Mirandese language, 9
Modern Portugal, 34–35
Monarchy, 29, 30
    abolishment, 32
    constitutional, 31
Monastery of Our Lady of Pena, 57
Monument of the Discoveries, 63
Moors, 23–27, 54, war of reconquest with27
    influence of, 25
Mountains, 14
Museu Municipal, 77
Music, 54

N
National
    Monument, 75
    Pantheon, 69
Nethera, 45
Netherlands, 37
Noah, 79
Nobel Prize for Literature, 54

O
Oliveira, Mateua Vicente de, 66
Olive oil, 38
Oliveria Salazar, António de, 32, 33, 34

P
Palace of
    Quelez, 66–67
    Sintra, 56–57
Palacio da Pena, 56, 57
Pastiés de nata, 52
Pedro II, 32
Peneda-Gerês National Park, 10
People, 9, 49–61
Pessoa, Frenando, 54
Philip II, 30
Phoenicians, 23
Pico Island, 15
Pomarão dam and hydroelectric power station, 82
Ponta
    Delgada, 44, 46
    do Pico (Pico or Pico Alto), 7
Population, 9
    age, 9
    growth rate, 9
    homogeneous, 49
Port, 38
Port
    of Leixões, 88
Porto, 17, 26, 44, 58, 63, 71–73, 74
    Cathedral, 72
    Santo, 46
Portuguese
    Bean Stew, 52–53
    language, 9, 51
    stick combat, 58
Praça
    do Bocage, 79
    do Comércio, 68
    Luis de Camões, 77
Praia da Marinha, 16
President, 34
Prime minister, 34, 35
Protestantism, 55
Public sector, 88

Q
Queima das Fitas (Burning of Ribbons), 50
Quinta do Lorde, 14

R
Real Madrid, 60
Recipes, 52–53
Religion, 9, 27, 55, 58
    freedom of, 58

94

INDEX

Republic, 8, 31
Resources, natural, 42
Rivers, 13, 17
Robillon, Jean-Baptiste, 67
Roman Catholicism, 9, 55
Romans, 23, 49, 54, 79
Ronaldo, Cristiano, 60
Russia, 61

S

Sado River, 39, 79
Santa
    Cruz Monastery (Monastery of the Holy Cross), 75
    Maria de Belém, 62
Saramago, José, 54
Seaports, 44
Serra da Estrela
    mountains, 14, 58
    Natural Park, 13
Sesimbra, 39
Setúbal, 44, 78, 79
Sierra de Sintra, 56
Silves, 25
Sinédrio, 31
Sines, 44
Sintra, 24, 56, 66
Soccer, 58, 60, 61
Socialist Party, 35
Solar panels, 84
Spain, 7, 11, 17, 29, 30, 42, 44, 45, 82
    invasion and annexation by, 30
Spanish language, 51
Speech, freedom of, 29
Sports, 58, 60, 61
St. George's Castle, 64, 65
Streetcars, 65
Subway, 44
Supreme Court, 35
Sweet Bread, 53

T

Tagus
    River, 7, 17, 22, 65, 68, 70
    Valley, 23
Tomar, 59
Torre mountain, 14
Tourism, 47, 80
Trade, 42
    routes, 13, 17, 29
Transportation, 44
Treaties of Rome, 37
Treaty of Paris, 37
Troubadours, 54
Tuna steak *(bife de atum)*, 52

U

Ukrainians, 49
UNESCO World Heritage Site, 62, 71
United
    Kingdom (UK), 42, 45
    States (US), 45, 81, 82
University of Coimbra, 76

W

Vasco da Gama Bridge, 70
Vicente, Gil, 54
Victoria, Queen, 57
Visigoths, 23, 49
Volcanoes, 15
Voting, 34

W

Wealth, 29, 30
West Germany, 36, 37
Wind turbines, 83, 84, 85
Wine *(vinhos)*, 38, 41, 52
World Cup, 61
World War
    I, 32
    II, 32, 36

Picture Credits

All images in this book are in the public domain or have been supplied under license by © Shutterstock.com. The publisher credits the following images as follows:
Page 6: Sergio TB, page 36: Roman Yanushevsky, page 37: Radu Bercon, page 50: De Visu, page 55: Filipe B Varela, page 59 Emily Marie Wilson, page 60: Marcos Mesa/Sam Wordley, page 61: Laszlo Szirtesi, page 64: StockPhotoArt, pages 66-67: Damira, page 73: Trabantos, page 67: Ross Helen, page 78: Nessa Gnatoush.
Wikimedia Commons and the following: page 78: Junta Informa.
To the best knowledge of the publisher, all images not specifically credited are in the public domain. If any image has been inadvertently uncredited, please notify the publisher, so that credit can be given in future printings.

Video Credits

Page 12 Visit Azores: http://x-qr.net/1FhJ
page 24 BEONBOARD _ORG: http://x-qr.net/1D8V
page 42 Nelson Carvalheiro: http://x-qr.net/1F65
page 51 Visit Portugal: http://x-qr.net/1Gdq
page 64 The New York Times: http://x-qr.net/1HdW

Author

Dominic J. Ainsley is a freelance writer on history, geography, and the arts and the author of many books on travel. His passion for traveling dates from when he visited Europe at the age of ten with his parents. Today, Dominic travels the world for work and pleasure, documenting his experiences and encounters as he goes. He lives in the south of England in the United Kingdom with his wife and two children.